# HOW TO DEAL WITH DIFFICULT PEOPLE

BEN NISSAN

INTRINSIC
PUBLICATIONS

PUBLISHED BY INTRINSIC PUBLICATIONS



Library and Archives Canada Cataloguing in Publication

Ben Nissan, author

How to Deal With Difficult People

| ISBN | VERSION |
|---|---|
| 978-1-7782254-3-7 | Book |
| 978-1-7782254-2-0 | Audio |
| 978-1-7782254-1-3 | Digital |
| 978-1-7782254-0-6 | Paperback |

INTRINSIC
PUBLICATIONS

www.projectintrinsic.com

# Table of Contents

# 1.

# Introduction

Have you ever had a negative interaction with someone and later regretted not having said or done the right thing to improve the interaction? Or worse, did you think that perhaps there was nothing you could have said or done to make it better?

You most likely have. This is a common and frustrating human experience. Frustrating enough, in fact, that few people like to dwell on such experiences, let alone relive them through painstaking analysis. Instead, most people dismiss the person or interaction and move on. They often do this by judging the person as being difficult, rude, etc. Although this judgement may capture a thin slice of reality, it is not helpful because it relieves one of responsibility and control when, in fact, there most likely was something that could have been said and/or done to improve the negative interaction. What was it? How can you know the right thing to say or do, reliably, across a multitude of highly varied circumstances and people? Is it always worth making an effort? When is avoidance or escape preferable to confrontation?

These are some of the questions that I try to answer in this short and to-the-point book. After all, these sorts of interactions are just like most things in the universe; they are patterned and, therefore, susceptible to analysis and strategy. Admittedly, the patterns are especially complex. But luckily, we are equipped with the kind of evolved biological hardware and software to handle it.

Some of us are better at it than others, but not entirely because of innate immutable qualities. Rather, because some people have developed better social, de-escalation, and negotiation skills; skills that can be honed. I can think of few skills that are more important. And yet, there is not a lot of material that deals directly with this topic. In my research, I came across bits and pieces rather than a synthesized whole. This book is my attempt to weave what are sometimes seemingly disparate concepts into a unified framework.

## A Bit About Me and My Approach

Admittedly, I never set out to write this book. It developed organically, out of necessity. Here is a bit of background about me to help you understand how I came to be interested in this topic.

Before attending law school and going on to become a lawyer, I completed a Bachelor's Degree in psychology. This alone would hardly qualify me to write competently about human behavior. However, it laid the foundations and nourished the seeds of interest that have continued to flourish to this day. Despite pursuing several other disciplines and life paths since my undergraduate days, including, to name a few, the aforementioned law career, music career, and serial entrepreneurship, I never stopped my personal research into human psychology. I estimate that I have completed over two thousand hours of reading and research on the topic in the last two decades. I kept up on the latest science, reading primary sources, research studies, books, and on occasion, conducting my own simple experiments. Perhaps just as importantly, I have been actively observing human behavior and discussing it with colleagues and friends, some of whom are experts in fields such as Clinical Psychology, Market Research, and Industrial-Organizational Psychology.

One of the things I do is run a Notary Public company. This company, as of the time of writing, has four locations across the province of Ontario, Canada, in four different cities. My job requires me and my fellow notaries to interact with the public on a regular basis. Together, we serve thousands of people a year from all walks of life. Most of our clients are pleasant to deal with. However, a small minority are difficult, aggressive, emotional, and even psychopathic.

I have come to realize that, in the course of over a decade of serving the public as a notary, I developed a methodical approach to dealing with clients that is based on the scientific research I am so passionate about. Out of necessity, I have taken the material from the pages I have read and applied it to both my personal and professional life. I have learned what works and what doesn't, at least for me.

It is in this professional context that, one day, a fellow notary asked me for some advice on how to deal with difficult clients. In response, I set out to draft a brief email to all the notaries in my company with a few tips on how I deal with difficult clients. I started with bullet points. The bullet points quickly grew into paragraphs. The paragraphs grew into pages. This made me realize that this is a rich topic that merits further work. Hence this book.

Before I proceed, please note a few things. First, I have substantially simplified many of the concepts I discuss as well as my overall approach. The benefit of this is that the material will be accessible. My goal is for anyone of any level of education, background, and expertise to be able to use these ideas and apply them in practical ways. The problem, of course, is that simplification can distort reality. I acknowledge that humans are complicated and that the interactions between them can give rise to dynamics that are too complex to model accurately. However, all that we can do is utilize theoretical frameworks of varying degrees of complexity and accuracy to navigate the world of human interaction. This book describes one such framework. My suggestion is to consume these ideas with an open mind and draw from it what you think will be helpful to you.

Second, and related to the first point, I have narrowed the scope of this book significantly. There are many sub-topics and related issues that could be discussed, which I have omitted because I want this book to be as concise as possible so that anyone can get through it quickly and start applying it right away.

Finally, although I have a passion for and a degree in psychology, I am not a vetted expert. I have not conducted my own peer-reviewed research (with the exception of my bachelor's degree thesis). These are my personal observations and insights—synthesized and woven together with research I have found to be compelling.

That said, it works. I can't know for certain that it will work for you, but it is my hope that you will find at least one concept, technique, or insight that will help you to deal with the difficult people in your life. The tips and techniques I will describe may be useful to you not only with clients or customers in professional settings but also with people in general in any type of interaction or relationship.

# 2.

# Behavioral Drivers

The first thing I do when I am faced with a difficult individual, or any individual for that matter, is determine what motivates them and drives their behavior. This is not an easy task but there are some perspectives and concepts that I find useful in this regard.

I prefer to think that most people are good by nature and that antisocial or aggressive behavior is the result of context or a system designed to incentivize or promote such behavior. This is a view shared by the preeminent doctor, Gabor Mate. He argues that humans have been physiologically wired for altruism and cooperation by evolution. This explains why it feels good to be good to others. That said, the tendency to be good to others can be hijacked by incentives that lead us to depart from our nature. There are plenty of studies in support of this view. The most notable and infamous are the Milgram experiments, where Stanley Milgram was able to convince ordinary individuals to torture strangers, simply by creating an illusion of authority.

Therefore, my initial instinct when interacting with a stranger is to give the benefit of the doubt. Much of the behavior we don't want to see in others is driven by fear, anxiety, pain, depression, etc., all of which can be exacerbated by circumstances outside the individual's control. Therefore, I rarely view any person as my challenger or enemy. Rather, I view the circumstances that have led to their transgression against me as our shared challenge. I don't think of other people's problems as separate from my own. So long as chance is operative in the universe, any problem that exists out in the world could cross paths with my experience. And when it does, I view it as my responsibility to respond to it in some way (or not, which is a decision in itself).

The decisions we make can be viewed hierarchically, with some being more optimal (i.e., more aligned with our goals) than others. Therefore, we ought to try and make the best ones we can. The alternative is to surrender to futility, which is unhelpful. Sometimes people develop the perspective that their thoughts and actions are meaningless, ineffectual, or pointless. Few things, in my opinion, are as destructive as this perspective. Your thoughts and actions affect reality (and vice versa), therefore, choose them wisely.

## Identifying Behavioral Drivers

My goal of understanding people's motivations usually leads me to examine the context for clues as to what is driving the problematic behavior. It just so happens that, in most cases (especially in a professional environment), the most salient and powerful contextual variable is other people, which of course includes me. That means that if someone isn't behaving well, I will first examine my own behavior. What have I said? What is my vocal tone and body language like? What is my physical position in the room relative to the person I am interacting with?

If I notice an issue with my own behavior, I will attempt to correct it. Of course, I am not always successful at accomplishing this. There are times when I fail to fully control my emotions, so they manifest themselves in my facial expressions, body language, voice, and actions. Even subtle expressions can be detected by others. And this can, at times, worsen a situation. On the other hand, there are times when displaying emotion is expected, useful, and even necessary.

That said, over the course of many years, I have improved my ability to remain calm and rational, enabling me to avoid negative emotions that can worsen a tense situation. Some people are naturally better at this than others. It didn't come naturally to me. It took a lot of work in my late teens and twenties to cultivate a calm demeanor that today has become a fully integrated part of who I am. Some of the things that helped me improve my emotional regulation include the practice of meditation, studying non-violent communication, a commitment to becoming more self-aware, a deliberate and concerted effort of feeling compassion toward others, being physically active, and the mitigation of my own ego.

When examining my own behavior for clues as to what may be driving someone else's behavior, I recognize the fact that my own behavior does not have to be inherently problematic to cause an issue. For example, there is nothing inherently wrong with smiling and making eye contact with someone when you greet them. In fact, most people view this as a friendly gesture. However, it is possible to encounter people that don't react well to this, either because of cultural differences, social anxiety, and/or personal idiosyncrasies. Sometimes, less smiling and less eye contact is better. It depends on the person as not everyone will react in the same way to the same stimulus. This is an easy concept to glaze over, so I want to emphasize it. Positive interactions with others require us to be sensitive to people's specific needs and idiosyncrasies. This is like the concept that to treat people equally, we sometimes have to treat people differently. This means that we must tailor our approach to suit the individual with whom we are interacting.

For example, some people like small talk—in fact, they need it to enter their zone of comfort. While others want to get right to the point. Similarly, some people want to be guided and even controlled or dominated, while others want to have all the control and to dictate the pace and manner of events. There are times when it's beneficial to cede control and times when it is better to hold onto it, to the benefit of all involved.

Further, some individuals will consistently blame themselves when things go wrong, even when there is evidence to the contrary. While others will consistently place the blame outside of themselves (e.g., the weather, the government, the person they are talking to), even when there is evidence to the contrary. By becoming aware of these sorts of differences, you can tailor your approach to the individual with whom you are interacting. In a sense, to get along with as many people as possible, it is important that we become adaptable social chameleons. This does not mean that we should change the core of who we are (i.e., personality, values, morals, etc.) in order to accommodate others. In fact, it is important that we remain genuine and true to ourselves. However, it does mean displaying a different pattern of behavior when it makes sense to do so. After all, we are not necessarily what we do, unless we make it a long-term habit that touches fundamental parts of our lives. Our actions, in isolation, don't define our core being.

For example, I have a friend I would describe as calm and patient across many contexts, including how he drives. However, on a trip to Brazil, I witnessed my friend drive very differently than in the past. He wasn't calm. He drove aggressively to fit in with the flow of traffic, etiquette, and expectations of Brazilian drivers. This temporary change in behavior didn't transform my friend into a permanently aggressive driver, let alone into an aggressive person. Temporary changes in the pattern of our behavior do not change who we are at our core. Rather, they allow us to adapt to our ever-changing circumstances.

Furthermore, there are many forms of behavior that do not inform or affect the core of who we are. Take, for example, how you brush your teeth. There are multiple techniques and types of toothbrushes. Perhaps it could be argued that the way you brush your teeth might offer a vague glimpse into your personality (it's a stretch), however, I don't think anyone would argue that if you changed the way you brush your teeth, it would change your personality, at least not directly. In the same way, changing other aspects of your behavior does not inevitably change who you are at your core.

I hope that it is clear by now that there is no single set of behaviors I can prescribe that will be useful to you in every situation with every person. You must cater to people's uniqueness. To do that, you must read them. And to do that quickly, especially with a stranger, you must free up as many cognitive resources as possible by relying on experience and mental shortcuts. All humans do this to some extent. Mental shortcuts, or "Heuristics" as it is known in the psychological literature, are an integral component of our mental faculties. Technically and broadly speaking, it is a form of categorization. And as you may know, the advantage of categorization is an increase in speed but with the sacrifice of accuracy. In the next sections, I will describe some of the heuristics that have been helpful to me.

## Mood Versus Disordered Temperament

It is important to distinguish between individuals that are difficult by nature due to their personality, and individuals that are difficult due to circumstance (perhaps due to being temporarily stressed). These two variables interact and influence one another, certainly. That is, some people's natural disposition may lead them to become more easily flustered by challenging circumstances than others. Conversely, a person's life circumstances can have an impact on their long-term outlooks and disposition. Nonetheless, I find it helpful to distinguish between two broad groups of difficult people and to cater my approach to each:

1) Ordinary people that are in a bad mood; and

2) People with personality disorders, particularly Antisocial Personality Disorder (also known as Psychopathy).

Happy, sad, fearful, hopeful, etc., are all examples of moods. Moods are temporary and fleeting. Some personality disorders, on the other hand, are permanent. Examples of personality disorders include the aforementioned Antisocial Personality Disorder (ASPD), Narcissism, Histrionic, Paranoid, Borderline, Avoidant, and Dependent. Some of these disorders are more treatable than others. Furthermore, they present varying degrees of challenge to the individuals that are suffering from them and to those that interact with them. An in-depth discussion of how to deal with each of these personality disorders is outside the scope of this book. Instead, I will focus on antisocial personality disorder, which I will refer to as psychopathy, and people that suffer from this disorder as psychopaths.

Generally speaking, moods are the least difficult to deal with, while psychopaths are the most difficult to deal with. The vast majority of difficult people you will encounter in your life are simply in a bad mood. Psychopaths, on the other hand, make up approximately 1% of our population, so it's rare that you will encounter one. Nonetheless, if you interact with a large number of people, as I do, chances are that you will eventually encounter a psychopath, so it's worthwhile to come up with strategies to deal with them. Furthermore, there are ancillary benefits to learning how to deal with a psychopath, even if you never encounter a psychopath in your lifetime. I will elaborate on this point later in the book.

The table below is a summary of how I approach members of each group:

| **People in a bad mood** | **Psychopaths** |
|---|---|
| Validate | Feign validation if useful only |
| Humanize yourself | Dehumanize yourself |
| Nurture | Do not nurture |
| Don't overwhelm | Overwhelm |
| Laugh and use humor | Don't laugh, unless useful |
| Empathize | Avoid empathizing |
| Mirror the positives only | Mirror everything (i.e., Game Theory's "tit for tat" approach) |
| Don't rely entirely on logic until they are calm enough to hear it | Use logic and rationality, even when they appear emotional |
| Be gentle and create a safe space | Be mildly hostile and threatening |
| Show vulnerability | Don't show vulnerability |
| Be open and honest | Deceive if needed |

As you can see, the social and psychological strategies I use are highly divergent and dependent on whether or not I am dealing with an ordinary person or a psychopath. How can you tell the difference between someone who is in a bad mood versus a psychopath? No one can offer an easy answer to this, but here are some rough guidelines:

- Assume that misbehavior is a result of a bad mood and circumstances, rather than psychopathy. Psychopaths are rare.
- Psychopaths seem fake when they display emotion, often because it *is* fake since they are not actually feeling the

emotion. They are only pretending to feel it because they have learned that it is useful to do so.

- Psychopaths usually derive enjoyment from causing pain to others (i.e., sadism), whereas an ordinary person will feel shame, guilt, and remorse for hurting you.
- Look for micro-expressions of joy on the face of a psychopath when you express pain or suffering. You can do this by feigning pain and watching their face carefully. If you try to do this while you're actually suffering, then your chances of an accurate reading will diminish. Instead, fake it and watch their eyes. If you detect joy, it is evidence that you're dealing with a psychopath. I acknowledge that this is not always the case. Some people smile when they are feeling socially awkward or stressed. That doesn't make them psychopaths. However, these types of individuals, in my experience, also happen to be the kinds of individuals that clearly do not mean to cause you any harm. In other words, other than their awkward smile, it will be obvious that you are not dealing with a psychopath.
- Psychopaths are charming at first, and when they don't get what they want, they will quickly turn on you, whereas a person who is in a bad mood will usually be in a bad mood from the outset—nothing charming about them.
- Psychopaths are more likely to lie in absurd ways that are easily falsifiable and for no apparent reason at all. Lying is an intrinsically pleasurable process for them.
- I don't usually suggest relying on your gut feelings because our guts are too often wrong. I prefer evidence and logic. However, this is one area where our senses have evolved to a sufficient degree to help us. So, do trust your gut. If you're not a naturally paranoid or skeptical individual and someone gives you a bad feeling, there's probably a valid reason for it. However, if you find yourself feeling like this multiple

times a week with different individuals, then your psychopath-meter likely requires calibration and is not to be trusted.

# 3.

# How to Deal with People That Are in a Bad Mood

## Accentuate Your Humanity

People vary in their capacity to generate empathy for others and to view matters from a perspective other than their own. There are several factors that can make it more difficult to empathize, such as whether there is a perceived dissimilarity to the person or group in terms of culture, political affiliation, race, age, etc. Also, keep in mind that if the person is in physical or psychological pain, their ability to empathize, as well as their ability to think clearly, will diminish. Even feeling a chill due to a low ambient temperature can diminish a person's ability to be kind and empathetic. Recall the last time you had the flu. I bet that almost all you could think about was yourself. You probably didn't spend much time thinking about the plight of humans in far-away places, who might, under normal circumstances, garner your empathy and perhaps even action (e.g., in the form of a donation or assistance of some kind). That said, you probably didn't lose all of your capacity to empathize. If someone made a compelling enough argument, then you might allow their cause and your empathy to pierce through the veil of your fever. You can be empathetic when you're in pain, it just takes more work to get you there. And the more pain you are in, the more work will be required.

By reminding people of your shared humanity, you can make it more likely that they will empathize with you or your position, or at the very least, that they will remain respectful and sensitive to your experience despite your disagreement. There are many ways in which you can do this. I discuss some specific techniques below.

Finally, before I proceed, it is important to note the difference between manipulation and influence. Manipulation results in a gain to the manipulator at a direct cost to the person being manipulated. Influence results in a gain for the person being influenced, and sometimes also for the person doing the influencing.

## Mirroring

Monkey see, monkey do. That's because our primate brains contain mirror neurons. When these neurons fire, it urges us to mimic the behavior of others. These are the same neurons that activate when you feel "pain" because of seeing someone else (particularly if it's someone you love) smash their thumb with a hammer.

This mental function is an adaptive response since it prompts others into thinking that we are like them or that we belong to their group. You can hack this feature of our evolved cognitive function by mirroring people's body language, words, mannerisms, etc. Many of us do this naturally, especially with people we like. For example, if you watch two friends sitting together and having a lively conversation, you might notice that their legs are crossed in the same way (such that they mirror each other), their hands are at a similar height, etc. Furthermore, they will shift their bodies at roughly the same time. One person might initiate the movement and the other will quickly follow.[1] This is all done unconsciously.

---

[1] I find that mirroring breaks down during video meetings. This could, in part, explain why virtual meetings are not as satisfying or connective as in-person meetings.

A very simple and effective way of mirroring is to repeat the last few words of a person's sentence before starting your own. It not only shows them that you're listening and engaged but it also mirrors them in a direct and precise way.

Some people consider mirroring to be manipulative, and it certainly can be. I think the intention determines whether it is. If you mirror someone for the purpose of gaining something from them at their loss, then it is, in fact, manipulative. However, if your intention is to foster connection for the benefit of the relationship, then it is not manipulative per se.

Be careful with the behaviors you mirror. In most cases, it's best to only mirror positive or pro-social behaviors (behaviors you want others to repeat) and avoid mirroring negative behaviors (behaviors you want others to cease). Furthermore, people are sometimes unaware of their actions. Imagine, for example, a person that is nervously fidgeting with their hands. They might not even be aware that they are doing it. If you mirror that behavior, it will escalate the tension in the room and thereby worsen the situation. Therefore, sometimes it's best not to mirror and instead opt to model the behavior you want to promote. I will discuss that next.

## Modelling

"Modelling" in this case refers to setting an example of the behavior you want to promote. This is most effective in circumstances where you have some authority and if you can exude confidence while doing it. This is a sort of reverse mirror.

For example, I use modelling to dictate the pace of speech in a conversation. I often encounter clients that speak very quickly, interrupt me, and can't deliver information in a concise and effective manner. I think that this is partly a result of anxiety and living in a fast-paced environment. It's also partly the result of momentum. That is, many clients arrive to our office moments after having driven a car. Driving is stressful and fast. Drivers are surrounded by thousand-pound machines that can kill them at any moment. Even if they are not psychologically aware of it, their bodies enter a mild fight-or-flight mode during driving. Their amygdala is firing.[2] They are stressed. It requires a level of hyper-alertness that persists beyond the trip, which sometimes hinders calm contemplation of information.

This fast pace is problematic because, in an effort to think and speak quickly, people make mistakes. I noticed this early on in my legal practice. I would catch myself getting swept away in my clients' momentum. Consequently, I would speak quickly too. That was a mistake. I have since learned that I should not allow my clients to dictate the pace and emotional tone of our meetings, unless the tone is largely positive. Now when I meet a client that is in a hurry, I slow down to a pace that is slower than my usual pace of speech. I slow down enough that the disparity between our paces becomes absurd and uncomfortable. Most people fix this dissonance by slowing down to match my pace. This helps them in the long run because it makes both them and me less likely to make a mistake. It improves our ability to actively listen and often has a calming effect.

If it doesn't work and they don't slow down, I ask them to slow down. I often start by asking them if they are in a hurry. If they say that they are, I usually respond with something like, "I am going to try to do this as quickly as I can but I don't want us to make a mistake. If we make a mistake, you'll need to come back and pay again and I don't want you to have to do that. Let's take our time and get this right. Do you have 10 minutes to go through this with me and get it right? If not, you should come back some other time."

I apply a similar approach with people that are rude or unprofessional. That is, I elevate my level of professionalism and

[2] The amygdala is a region of the brain that deals with emotions, particularly fear.

formality to an almost absurd degree. I want the person I am speaking with to experience the disparity between us. This often results in a cognitive dissonance that is uncomfortable and usually leads the person to match me or at least to rise to a higher level of civility than they are accustomed to. I am sometimes surprised at how well this works. Most people know what good manners and courtesy look like—they just need a reminder and for someone to model it.

One of the ways that this helps my clients is that it makes them more likeable to me, which, in turn, makes me more likely to want to help them. No matter how hard I try, it's difficult for me to muster the same level of energy and enthusiasm to help someone that is irritating me.

## Eye Contact

Whether or not our eyes are, in fact, the window to our souls is irrelevant. What matters is that many people perceive this to be true, whether they are conscious of it or not. What matters even more is that research has shown that eye contact alone is sufficient to build rapport, and even a bond, between strangers. There are several reasons for this having to do with how our brains develop as infants, our social heuristics, and our sense of self. A comprehensive discussion on this topic falls outside the scope of this book. For now, it suffices to state that it does work.

Be careful, however, about making too much eye contact. As with all good things, you have to find the right balance. That's something you gauge on a case-by-case basis. As a rough rule of thumb though, women require more eye contact than men and extroverts require more eye contact than introverts.

Eye contact can be a social lubricant for an entirely different reason than building rapport. It lets the person know that they are being watched; that they are seen; that they are not anonymous.

People are more likely to misbehave if they believe they can get away with it.[3]

This has been illustrated in many studies, including one conducted by Melissa Bateson and colleagues at Newcastle University, UK. In this particular study, people in an office kitchen could purchase coffee on the basis of the honor system by dropping money into a box. The researchers created two conditions. In condition A, the price list contained an image of a flower, whereas, in condition B, the price list contained an image of a human eye. As you might guess, condition B collected more money from the office workers (2.7 times more, in fact). The researchers concluded that even an image of an eye is sufficient to make people feel like they are being watched, and therefore, less likely to cheat by underpaying for the coffee. This effect works in conjunction with the Priming Effect, which I discuss next.

## Priming

Priming is a powerful and well-studied phenomenon. It occurs when one stimulus influences a person's response to a different stimulus.

The best way to understand the concept and power of priming is to examine some examples. One of the most famous, and now somewhat controversial, priming studies involved splitting people into two groups.[4] In one group, people were told a fictional story

---

[3] Anonymity is part of what explains road rage and nastiness in online communication.

[4] The original study was published in 1996. A later study attempted to replicate the results in 2012 but was unsuccessful. The difficulty in replicating the original study may stem from an expectancy bias (that of the researchers and participants, all of whom may have been familiar with the original study). It should be noted that the field of psychology research as a whole is currently suffering from a replication crisis. Nonetheless, priming as an effect is well supported by thousands of studies. Though some of the specific studies on priming may be controversial, priming itself is not.

about elderly characters. The other group was told a story about young characters. The researchers found that the group that was told the story about the elderly characters, on average, walked out of the research lab more slowly than the group that was told a story about young characters. Presumably, thinking about the elderly made people feel older and resulted in a slower pace.

In another study, participants were given a choice between a healthy snack (radish) and an unhealthy snack (cookie). Before being given the choice, participants walked to the room through a hallway that contained either images of fit-looking people living a healthy lifestyle (e.g., exercising) or images of unhealthy-looking people engaged in unhealthy behaviors. On average, as you might guess, participants that walked through the hallway with the healthy images were more likely to choose the healthy snack as compared to participants that walked through the hallway with unhealthy images.

A collaborative study by researchers at Harvard, MIT, and Yale found that when rating a stranger's personality, participants were more likely to form a warmer impression of the stranger if they were holding a hot cup of coffee in their hands compared to participants that held a cup of iced coffee in their hands.[5]

That's priming. There are many types. A general lesson we can draw from the priming effect is that subtle cues in the environment can nudge our behavior in one direction or another. Knowing this can allow you to use priming as a tool.

For instance, you can prime clients to include you in their perceived group by broadening the category of the group so that it includes both of you in it (e.g., "Canadian", "a hard-working professional", "human", "a person with a family", etc.). You can do this by using statements that refer to a shared experience. A

---

[5] https://science.sciencemag.org/content/328/5986/1712?sid=9a6810a0-0083-4a3b-9449-04d476d7e6d1

common example is to talk about the weather, particularly if the weather is harsh or challenging. A common challenge or threat, such as a storm, encourages unity and cooperation.

I sometimes pepper my conversation with clients with statements that start with "us Canadians…" or "us professionals". The use of the word "us" is effective so long as it includes both individuals.

Another example is to set up your physical environment in a clean and orderly manner. If your office is messy, clients will be more likely to misbehave and underperform. A tidy office signals that order is of value and that it must be heeded in this particular place. This conclusion is related to and strengthened by the broken windows theory, which states that visible signs of disorder, crime, and chaos increase the probability that people will engage in criminal or destructive behavior.

## Use Names

You can improve rapport by using a person's name. You probably already know this, but you most likely don't know why it works. I don't either. I tried to research this and, unfortunately, couldn't find any compelling studies. I found articles on the internet but the quality of analysis wasn't very good.

My speculation is that this works for some of the same reasons that eye contact works. That is, it mitigates the issues that arise with anonymity. When you use a person's name, you're telling them that you know who they are. Therefore, the more evidence you gather about their identity, the more likely they are to behave in a prosocial manner. Secondly, by using a person's name, you bias them into including you in their tribe. Our friends and family members call us by our first names. So, when you use a person's name, you are triggering a Pavlovian association. Just as Pavlov's dogs salivated at the sound of a bell due to its association with food, perhaps people warm up to others that use their name due to the association with the broad group "non-stranger".

As with some of the other techniques I've discussed, be careful not to overdo this. Once or twice is often enough. Overuse could appear manipulative or even dominating. Imagine if someone said your name prior to starting every sentence. I can't imagine a scenario where this would go well.

## Ask "How" Questions

I love questions. They are powerful, for many reasons, including the fact that they open pathways to information. Furthermore, questions encourage the person you are speaking with to reason through an issue in accordance with your framing. This, in turn, can encourage empathy.

Avoid questions that begin with "why" and invoke a "you" (for example, "Why did you do this?") as those are often viewed as hostile and challenging. Whereas questions that begin with "How" and invoke your own experience (for example, "How can I accept this?") are perfectly reasonable to ask and they often require the person you're speaking with to take your perspective and to solve your problem for you. A "How" question is especially useful when someone asks you to do something you can't or don't want to do. If a client makes a lame attempt at answering your "how" question by saying something like "you just do it", then it merits an assertive rejection.

It is also important to ask yourself questions. The benefits of self-confidence get a lot of attention in our society. However, self-doubt can be beneficial too. Perhaps now, more than ever, we need more self-doubt. It's a cornerstone of humility after all. We can be both confident in one moment and self-doubting in another.

## Use Humor

Humor can deescalate a tense situation, help form a social bond, and reduce stress levels. High stress causes your body to release the stress hormone cortisol, which impedes cognition. So, in a way, if you make someone laugh, you make them smarter.

That said, use it only when it's proper to do so. Whether or not it's proper depends on the situation and who you are. That's right, who you happen to be matters a great deal. Furthermore, humor should not be used in a dispassionate or contrived manner. It must come from a real place. Therefore, if the casual use of humor is not already part of your personality or communication repertoire, be careful how you use it. If it feels forced or contrived, don't do it. Instead, focus on cultivating your sense of humor gradually and patiently over many months or years. Practice with the nice clients or people in your life. Once you've figured out a smooth way to inject it into daily conversation, then you can try to apply it in a tense situation.

## Get Them to Name the Emotion

Research has shown that identifying what you are feeling and naming the emotion can enable you to mitigate its negative effects. You probably already utilize this technique to some extent. Perhaps when you are not feeling well, you ask yourself questions such as "what am I feeling? What is making me feel this way?". This form of contemplation, though seemingly simple, can be effective at helping you manage your emotions.

Not everyone is taught to do this though and not everyone has the emotional intelligence to figure it out on their own. Therefore, if you encounter a client that is having a tough time dealing with their emotions, you can help them gain control by asking them to pay attention to what they are feeling. I realize that this can be awkward to do in a professional setting (unless you're in a therapy session). "What are you feeling?" is not a broadly acceptable question in social settings, unfortunately. However, there are ways to make it less awkward or invasive. Much depends on your phrasing. Here are a few examples that have worked for me in the past:

"You seem upset. Are you upset?"
"Are you upset with me?"
"You seem frustrated, are you?"
"You don't seem very happy right now. What is going on?"
"I want this to be a positive interaction. What is preventing us from making that happen?"

The purpose of these questions is to help guide the client's awareness to his internal state. This can turn a bad conversation into a positive or even enjoyable one. I have experienced this in my life many times. I have witnessed clients transition from shouting at me to apologizing and thanking me on their way out the door. Getting people to make this transition requires tact, effort, and patience. There are times when I don't feel like doing it. Times when I am tempted to shout back. I'm an emotional being too. But I remind myself that nothing good comes from a shouting match.

## Validate

Most people know when they've gone off the rails and lost control. Yet, some continue their outburst of emotion despite this knowledge because they are often powerless to stop it. Negative powerful emotions are physiologically and psychologically draining.[6]

---

[6] There are exceptions. Anger, for example, can be energizing in the short term and, partly for this reason, addictive.

When someone enters a draining negative cycle, whatever small amount of energy and cognitive capacity remains will become devoted to saving face. We are social animals. We don't want to appear mean, fragile, unintelligent, etc. If you witness someone "lose it", it's your moral duty as a fellow human to help that person break their negative emotional spiral. You can do this by helping them feel less ashamed of themselves. Shame is harmful. One way to do this is by validating their emotions. You might be tempted to also compliment the person; don't. Compliments release feel-good chemicals, such as dopamine, that are like naturally occurring cocaine in the brain. This can reinforce the behavior.

How to validate? Here are three ways:

1. Relate. You can do this by telling an anecdote about a time when you or someone that you love and respect went through a similar situation and felt similarly. Be careful, however, not to speak for too long or in-depth on the matter to avoid making the conversation about you.
2. Let the person know that you understand what they are going through and that it's ok. Repeat, rephrase, and reframe their statements.
3. Ask a question; the sort of question that allows the person to build on their story.

Shame is everyone's enemy. But don't conflate shame with guilt. I view feelings of "guilt" as largely beneficial. Guilt is corrective; shame is destructive. A good way to understand the difference between shame and guilt is to think of feelings of shame as "I am bad" and guilt as "I did something bad". Again, we are not our actions. Having done something bad does not necessarily make you a bad person.

By the way, this distinction is also helpful to keep in mind when attempting to provide constructive feedback. If you tell someone that they are bad then you're merely criticizing them, which won't get you anywhere. Instead, mentally and verbally separate people's behavior from who they are and criticize their actions. You can disagree with someone's actions and yet continue to love and care for them and think of them as a good person.

## Clarify Your Intent

People sometimes say things without thinking about what it is that they hope to accomplish with their statements. My theory is that part of the reason for this is that some words, phrases, and sentences simply sound good. They have a ring to them. They might rhyme or have a pleasing cadence. This is partly the reason that we enjoy things like poetry, lyrics, and literature. It could be argued that language has an intrinsic value, rather than merely being a means to an end.

Another reason may be that a particular statement was useful to the speaker at some point in the past. Or, similarly, that statement was made to them in the past and they found it compelling. Let's call this Statement Recycling. People recycle statements because it saves time and energy. Humans are adapted to plug energy holes. Thinking through every word requires energy. So, we end up taking shortcuts.

Although this is understandable, it is usually counterproductive in the long run, particularly in the context of difficult conversations. If you want to explore the joy of language in an uninhibited fashion, it is best to do so in a friendly conversation where both parties are aware of what is happening. When having a difficult conversation, however, it is best to refrain from thoughtless regurgitations of phrases and sentences because, in the long run, they cause more harm than good.

In the context of a difficult conversation, I often ask myself, "why do I want to say what I am about to say? What do I want to accomplish with this statement? What do I want the listener to feel, think, or do?" If you get in the habit of doing this, you'll find that you sometimes don't have a good reason for saying what you want to say. Even worse, sometimes what you want to say is counterproductive or inconsistent with your goals. Sometimes you have to admit to yourself that you're simply angry and you want to hurt the listener. If that's the case, it's best not to proceed.

If, on the other hand, you are able to commit to positive intentions in a difficult conversation, then it is useful to let the other person know about your intent. Sentences such as "I am trying to help you" and "I want to find a way to make this work for both of us" tend to deescalate tense situations and foster collaboration.

## What is Empathy?

Unfortunately, empathy is a convoluted concept. Furthermore, there are different, sometimes contradictory, definitions of empathy. I will do my best to untangle this conceptual mess, at least for the purposes of this book. You might not like my definitions, but the actual definitions are not important. It's the concepts that I am seeking to build with them that are important.

I define empathy as a complex cognitive process that includes all the following elements:

1) Theory of mind;
2) Feeling another person's emotions; and
3) Responding appropriately to another person's emotions.

Theory of mind requires that a person have a sense (or theory) of what another person is feeling and thinking through personal observation. For example, if Bob sees Anna frowning, Bob could develop the theory that Anna is feeling sad. Not everyone has a good theory of mind. For example, people with autism can have difficulties forming beliefs about other people's states of mind.

Importantly, this does not mean that individuals with autism do not care about other people or that they lack compassion. On the contrary, when autistic individuals become explicitly aware of other people's suffering, they are as motivated as anyone to help alleviate the suffering.

However, when an individual has a good theory of mind, they will, in most cases, feel some of the same feelings to one degree or another (usually to a substantially lesser degree). Psychopaths fail at this stage. They cannot feel other people's emotions, despite having theory of mind.

People that have theory of mind and feel other people's emotions are often compelled, by their own feelings, to respond in an appropriate manner. In contrast, a psychopath's drive to respond is fueled by his desire to manipulate.

Empathy is not always a good thing. There are times when sympathy or "controlled empathy" is more appropriate. **Sympathy** is caring about and understanding the suffering of others without necessarily feeling other people's emotions or personally observing other people's emotions. I would argue that Sympathy does not require theory of mind. I can have sympathy for individuals that I have never met but have some second-hand knowledge of. Sympathy stems from a more general love and care for all sentient beings. After all, humans can care about the feelings and circumstances of people they have never met. This kind of caring is often informed by socio-cultural norms and values.

**Controlled empathy** entails having a theory of mind, avoiding feeling the person's emotions, and yet caring about the person's emotions. Kind of like a psychopath that cares. It is a bit tricky to pull off, but it is certainly possible. In fact, this is what good therapists do. They listen, understand the emotions of their clients, and yet remain emotionally neutral enough to assist their clients. It would be a failure for a therapist to deeply feel her client's emotions.

Imagine a therapist that curls up into the fetal position and bursts out in tears as she listens to her client's story. It is possible that the therapist may do something like this after the session but certainly not during the session.

In a professional setting such as the workplace, sympathy or controlled empathy is often what you want to aim for, not empathy. This is especially the case in conflict situations. That is, you should care about the conflict and about the experience your client is going through, but you should not deeply feel their emotions. By staying calm and largely, though not entirely, unemotional, you will be in a much better state to brainstorm solutions and to help keep the client calm. I know that this is much easier said than done. Sometimes I get emotional even when I know that it won't help me. I'm human, not a machine. That said, the duration of the emotion can be reduced through practice, especially in conjunction with meditation. In most cases, the ability to control the duration and/or expression of an emotion makes all the difference. Therefore, it is helpful to have an emotional outlet available to you.[7] I do not recommend bottling up emotions indefinitely. I do, however, recommend deferring their expression to a later point in the day when needed.

In contrast, when someone is experiencing positive emotions around you, it's beneficial to empathize with them and to feel their emotions. It allows a positive synergy to form, thereby enabling positive emotions to resonate and grow. Empathy is also necessary in situations where someone you love is expressing negative emotions that don't have a practical solution. For example, when someone is grieving the loss of a loved one. In a case like this, sympathy may not be sufficient. On the other hand, if you're not

[7] Here are some examples: exercise, hug from a loved one, a crying session, entering a state of flow by doing something you love such as playing a musical instrument, meditation, yoga, sauna, cold water.

very close to the person that is grieving and you never had a relationship with the deceased, then sympathy might be more appropriate, whereas empathy might be perceived as strange or disingenuous. Imagine going to a funeral where you did not know the deceased, nor are you close to his closest friends and family members, and yet you are the one crying the loudest and displaying the most emotion. It could work if crying loudly is part of your personality, but it would nonetheless be perceived by others as strange and inappropriate.

The table below summarizes the concepts I discussed in this section:

| | Theory of Mind | Feeling other's emotions | Responding to others due to own feelings | Responding to others due to norms and values | Responding to others to manipulate |
|---|---|---|---|---|---|
| Empathy | x | x | x | x | |
| Sympathy | | | | x | |
| Psychopathy | x | | | | x |
| Autism | | | x | x | |
| Controlled Empathy | x | | | x | |

## Conclusion

All the frameworks and techniques I have discussed so far have an overarching principle: that we should help others maintain or reach an emotional equilibrium for the benefit of all. The goal is a win-win. I would go as far as to argue that we have a moral obligation to do so, though this argument falls outside the scope of this book. Furthermore, it is not a necessary argument because I hope that, by now, you can appreciate the fact that, at the very least, such an approach has obvious practical benefits.

In the next section, I'll discuss several techniques designed to help ourselves, not the other. Sometimes at the cost of the other. The goal is to win at all costs to the other.

# 4.

# How to Deal with a Psychopath

Recall that early on in this book, I drew a distinction between individuals that are difficult to deal with due to circumstance or mood versus individuals that suffer from personality disorders. So far, I have talked about how to deal with the former. This next section will cover my perspective on how to deal with people that have personality disorders, particularly psychopathy.

## What is a Psychopath?

There is not an agreed-upon definition of a psychopath. It's a complex disorder that requires nuanced understanding. To make matters worse, the word "psychopath" has been misunderstood on a cultural level, mostly due to its use in popular media. The media portrays psychopaths as out-of-control violent killers. This isn't entirely accurate because lack of control and murder are not the hallmarks of this disorder. Most psychopaths never kill anyone.

When I use the word psychopath, I am referring to the more clinical sense of the word. That is, an individual that, among other things, is unable to empathize with others. This is the central trait of psychopaths in my opinion. Psychopaths also tend to be superficially charming, male[8], prone to lying, sadistic (deriving joy

[8] It is for this reason that I use the "he/him" gender pronouns when referring to psychopaths.

from the pain of others), promiscuous, egocentric, and manipulative. In my view, however, these traits, with the exception of sadism, are simply symptoms of the combination of lacking empathy and living in a competitive environment.

Psychopathy is considered to be a personality disorder. In many ways, it is also a physiological disorder. Psychopaths' brains are wired differently. Recent research has shown that their inability to empathize actually stems from a cognitive deficit that is correlated with brain damage, which may have occurred early in life. It is worth pointing out, therefore, that psychopaths are not to be hated. In fact, they should be pitied. They are the way they are due to causes outside of their control. This is a point I alluded to at the outset of this book. Hate is not a useful emotion. Rather, it is a byproduct of other useful emotions such as anger, fear, and discrimination.[9] Therefore, psychopaths should have our pity. They are as much victims of their own psychological and physiological reality as anyone.

To make matters worse, psychopathy is one of the very few disorders that is resistant to treatment. Psychology has made many advancements in recent years with a multitude of techniques, such as cognitive-behavioral therapy, to successfully treat, or at least mitigate, a wide variety of disorders. However, nothing seems to work with psychopaths. Once a psychopath, always a psychopath.

Psychopaths reveal a lot about human relationships and society at large. They teach us that without empathy, our social structure would not work. Emotion, caring, love, does indeed make the world

[9] I am not referring here to racial or gender discrimination, as the word "discrimination" often evokes. I am referring to the root of the word, as in to find a difference among two things. For example, the difference between a fresh and a rotten strawberry. Discrimination often necessitates categorization between things we love and hate. For example, I love fresh strawberries and I hate rotten strawberries. Therefore, it is useful for me to discriminate against rotten strawberries.

go round. I strongly believe that if we all lived like volcans or cybernetic systems that don't emulate emotion, we would not collaborate in the manner that we do, which ultimately would lead to the demise of our species.

## Why You Should Care

As I have stated several times, psychopaths are rare. It is unlikely you will have to closely interact with one. Why then should you make an effort to learn about how to deal with psychopaths? There are at least two good reasons I can think of. The first is that cultivating your psychopath strategy will make you a better person. I'll expand on this point later as it will form one of the central points of this book.

The second reason you should care about how to deal with psychopaths is risk management. Here, I am borrowing from the risk assessment rationale of actuarial science. When assessing risk and your potential response to that risk, it is not sufficient to merely assess the probability that something will or won't happen. You must also factor in the potential harm it can cause and the cost of mitigation. For example, if the probability of an event is high, the potential harm is high, and the cost of mitigating it is low, then the obvious choice is to mitigate the harm. An example of this is crossing a busy street. The chance of getting hit by a car is high, the potential harm is substantial (it could kill you), and mitigation (i.e. using a crosswalk, looking both ways before crossing) is not very costly. This sort of analysis is the justification behind things such as paying for insurance. For example, it is unlikely that your house will catch fire and burn down, however, if that were to happen, then it would have a major negative impact on your life. Therefore, you get insurance, as long as the cost of insurance is low enough.

If we apply this reasoning to the risk posed by psychopaths, it would look like this: the probability of encountering a psychopath is low, the amount of potential harm is high, and the cost of pre-emptively preparing for this and mitigating the harm from a psychopath is moderate. Therefore, ask yourself if you're willing to pay a moderate cost (your time and effort) for learning how to improve your chances at thwarting a potentially high degree of harm from a rare circumstance. Obviously, my personal calculation of this issue has led me to study and prepare for psychopaths extensively. And it has paid off several times.

## A Thought Experiment

Imagine that you have the choice between living in a universe designed by either of the following:

1) Someone that loves you
2) A stranger
3) Nature
4) A psychopath

Who or what would you choose? How would you rank these choices?

My choices are ranked in the order I listed above. Here is my reasoning: the people that love me, by definition, want the best for me. They would create a universe with laws that are least likely to cause me suffering. You might argue that humans are not qualified to create a universe and that, therefore, they would do a terrible job and inadvertently cause suffering. This may be, however, my frame of reference in this thought experiment is not with regard to the competence level of the creator, but rather the intention. Therefore, for the purposes of this thought experiment, assume that all the creators have the same level of competence in bringing their intention into reality. Thus, the only variable to consider in your evaluation is intention itself.

I chose a stranger above nature because even a stranger will have a bias toward wanting to mitigate the suffering of others. Humans, by default, have a sense of fairness and goodness. Societies, which are environments built by humans, are not perfect but they are more suitable to human life than the state of nature. It is for this reason that most people choose to live in a society, rather than in the wild.

Nature, on the other hand, is neutral. I think of nature's momentum as a powerful river. When it flows in the direction you want to go, it empowers you; when it intersects with your path, it destroys you. Humans (and some animals) are special because of our ability to empathize and our sense of fairness. All other intelligences, including the intelligence of nature, as contained in algorithmic processes such as evolution, as well as the artificial intelligence of computers, do not possess a sense of fairness. And neither does the psychopath.

The one major difference between nature and the psychopath, however, is that the psychopath is not perfectly neutral. On the contrary, the psychopath has a conscious agenda that is fueled by the primal structures of the human brain. The structures that evolved first, to deal with locomotion, bodily function, and, more problematically, base drives such as hunger, sex, power, resource acquisition, and domination. That is a problem because the primal parts of our brain are highly anti-social. Furthermore, and crucially, as is often the case, psychopaths derive pleasure from the suffering of others. Therefore, psychopaths are incentivized by their neurochemical cerebral environment to cause harm. That's why they are my last choice in this thought experiment.

In summary, the people that love us are most motivated to mitigate our suffering. Strangers are somewhat motivated to mitigate our suffering. Nature is neutral, as it does not contain a motivation to cause or mitigate suffering. Psychopaths are motivated to increase our suffering.

So, how do you deal with someone that is motivated to increase your suffering? I provided some guidelines earlier which I will now discuss in greater detail.

## Specific Techniques for Dealing with Psychopaths

### Feign Validation If Useful

The purpose of validation, in most cases, is to help others feel heard, mitigate any shame that they might feel, and foster bonding. These goals, however, shift when dealing with a psychopath. Helping a psychopath feel heard could be of value but note that they are unlikely to feel any shame and it isn't their goal—nor should it be yours—to bond.

Psychopaths learn that to get by in the world and get what they need, it is useful to pretend to be a normal human being with normal emotions and tendencies.[10] They will fake this. In most circumstances, even when you are certain that you are dealing with a psychopath, don't call their bluff. Let them fake it. A psychopath faking normalcy is preferable to a psychopath that is unhinged, so long as you don't let him manipulate you. Therefore, if you validate the psychopath, you'll be signaling that everything is ok and that you believe the psychopath is a normal person, thereby maintaining the charade. The hope here is that he will act normal, to your benefit.

---

[10] Please note that my use of the word "normal" here and throughout similar contexts in this book does not relate to any objective measure of normalcy. Rather, by "normal", I simply mean someone that is not a psychopath. I acknowledge that the word "normal" is problematic at worst and incoherent at best unless it is narrowly defined, as I have done here.

This having been said, there is a point at which it is important to call the psychopath's bluff; to let him know that you know he's trying to manipulate you. This threshold is reached when the attempted manipulation itself is harmful and you want to thwart the attempt. For example, imagine a scenario where a psychopath attempts to gain your trust by first befriending a mutual friend. Your friend, in this case, becomes an innocent bystander that may get hurt when the psychopath decides he no longer has a use for your friend. By letting the psychopath know that you know what he's up to, you're more likely to dissuade him from going down that path in the first place. After all, the psychopath will not want to waste his effort on someone that is difficult to manipulate.

It's a bit of a game. I dislike these sorts of games, but it is necessary when dealing with a psychopath. Furthermore, if you view it as a game and keep your cool, you will be more likely to win.

## Dehumanize Yourself

In most cases, your aim should be to end your interaction with a psychopath. If you need something from a psychopath, make sure it aligns with his goals, or avoid needing it. If you really need something from a psychopath, don't appeal to his humanity. Make a rational case and use carrots and sticks for leverage.

In most cases, dissuade the psychopath from interacting with you by making it less fun for him to interact with you. Sadism is a common trait among psychopaths. Rob him of the joy of making you suffer. If you dehumanize yourself then you will discourage him from inflicting pain on you. This strategy is often portrayed in movies, where the protagonist is being tortured and he pretends not to feel the pain. This is a poor strategy when dealing with a normal human but a good strategy when dealing with a psychopath.

An effective way to dehumanize yourself is to use your professionalism as a shield. Allow your personality and behavior to merge with the system, corporate entity, or office that you represent. Remove as much of the human element as possible. After all, abstract entities such as corporations are difficult to hurt in a traditional sense. For the psychopath, it is much more fun to hurt people than it is to hurt an abstract concept.

## Do Not Nurture

When you nurture a normal person who is in a bad mood, the hope is that this will soothe them sufficiently to enable them to collect their emotions and respond to you in a more rational, less angry way. This allows for a two-way communication and is to the benefit of everyone. I recommend doing this. A psychopath, on the other hand, isn't looking to hurt you because he's angry per se. Rather, he wants something from you, or he simply wants your pain as his pleasure. He won't respect or respond positively to your nurturing. He likely doesn't view nurturing as a rational behavior (and in some sense, it isn't). Act cold and he will be more likely to leave you alone.

## Don't Laugh

Laughter could be interpreted as gullibility, and therefore, vulnerability. Don't show this side of you to a psychopath. He will attempt to exploit it. Instead, persuade him that you are the kind of person that won't let her guard down. Dissuade him from attempting to manipulate you. There are exceptions, of course. You could laugh to feign a lack of fear or lack of caring. This can sometimes be useful. My point is that you should use it deliberately, as a tool, rather than genuinely in a moment of emotional abandon.

## Avoid Empathy

Empathizing with a psychopath poses several problems. First, empathizing is a very human thing to do, which violates one of the guidelines I discussed above. I suggest that you obscure your humanity as much as possible when dealing with a psychopath. Second, empathy evolved under conditions of reciprocity and cooperation amongst humans. Therefore, we have the expectation that empathy will be reciprocated. Psychopaths don't reciprocate. They can't. Which brings us to the third problem. Psychopaths do not feel their emotions in the same way that non-psychopaths do. Therefore, there is little for you to relate to and empathize with.

I realize that my views on this topic will be judged harshly by some. Particularly those that have a strict empathy-for-all policy. However, I think this is because people conflate love with empathy. I could be persuaded that everyone deserves some form of love, but I firmly believe that empathy, of the precise sort I defined earlier, is not helpful when dealing with psychopaths.

That said, one of the elements of empathy is helpful when interacting with a psychopath. Specifically, having theory of mind. Although it is difficult to form a theory of a mind that is substantially different from yours, you need to try because it will help you avoid getting duped and manipulated. Unfortunately, this will require you to play a mental game with the psychopath because he will lie to you and test you. Show him you know what he is up to. If he feigns an emotion and you fall for it, he will think that you are the kind of person that can be fooled and taken advantage of. I do not mind letting people think that I am a fool. In fact, sometimes I find it useful to play the role of the fool. However, it is not useful with psychopaths. It encourages them. Ironically, or perhaps appropriately, the best strategy against a psychopath is to feign psychopathy by showing little emotion and a willingness to manipulate. This takes us to the next section.

## Mirror Everything (Tit for Tat Strategy)

I spoke about mirroring earlier with regards to body language. Here, I am using it in a slightly different sense. It is not about body language per se. Rather, it is about how you respond to attacks and bids for cooperation. I am basing this strategy on the lessons we have learned from Game Theory research over the course of several decades. If you are not already familiar with Game Theory, I highly recommend reading about it. There is also a great Radiolab podcast on the topic.

The findings of Game Theory have been successfully utilized in a wide variety of contexts, including wars between nations, economics, video games, business, and even mechanism design. One of the big take-aways of Game Theory is that when you are dealing with an opponent in a zero-sum contest with imperfect information about the future and how someone might react, the best strategy is to attack when they attack and cooperate when they cooperate. This is called the Tit for Tat strategy. A slight variation of this approach is called the Generous Tit for Tat strategy, where you retaliate imperfectly (about 90% of the time) to encourage cooperation. This latter approach is my preferred strategy in most competitions. My goal, after all, is to foster as much cooperation as possible.

The main point I want you to draw from this section is that whenever you are dealing with a psychopath, it's a competition; it's never a cooperative process. And if you're going to compete it's often useful to apply the traditional Tit-for-Tat strategy, not the Generous Tit for Tat strategy. This will maximize your chances of winning against a psychopath.

## Be Mildly Hostile and Threatening

I do not recommend outright hostility and threats. Remain professional, composed, civil, but somehow drop some subtle hints that you are not the kind of person to be trifled with; you won't give up; you're a fighter. And if need be, you are just crazy enough to fight to the death. How do you do this? How do you politely let a person know that you will kill them if you have to? There is no single answer to this. It will depend on the context. Watch some mobster movies. Actors are great at conveying this. Pay attention to scenes where a seemingly nice guy in a nice suit is sharing a meal with another guy and, somehow, you know that if the situation requires it, the seemingly nice guy will flip over the table and pull out a gun. Be that guy, minus the gun. And only in self-defense. More on all this later.

## Recognize the Failure

A good idea expressed well, especially linguistically, is a powerful cultural force. That is, ideas on their own are not sufficient to alter culture. They must be expressed or utilized in some way in order to have an impact outside the mind. Words on their own are not sufficient either. They must be cohesive and backed by an idea that is compelling.

Despite this powerful combination or process, from an idea born in a mind to its expression in audible or legible language, we don't have a word or phrase for it. The closest word I can think of to describe this is a "meme". Not in the internet sense. Rather, in the original sense of the word, as coined by Richard Dawkins in his book, The Selfish Gene. Dawkins defined a meme as a noun that "conveys the idea of a unit of cultural transmission, or a unit of imitation". Just like genes, memes can have varying degrees of utility depending on the context. Thus, useful memes spread through replication (i.e., repetition) from person to person.

Words, ideas, memes, and genes have a lot in common with computers. In fact, one of the latest, and most successful, artificial intelligence techniques is called Neuroevolution. It utilizes multiple neural networks to solve a problem, and the ones that are most successful get to replicate with other networks (by combining their algorithmic information) and form new networks. Sound familiar?

It's procreation between algorithms. This process is repeated multiple times until a network is born that can adequately meet a desired outcome. But what does all this have to do with psychopaths?

Sometimes it helps me to think of people, particularly psychopaths, as being similar to computers in the sense that they can be programmed. Instead of computer code, we use human language. I should clarify here that I am not referring to the sort of programming associated with brainwashing and manipulation. I am referring to a softer, subtler form of programming. Every time you express a thought linguistically, or wave your hand, sing a song, wink, etc., and someone hears or sees it, you alter a small part of their neural structure. After all, memory formation and processing in the human brain is a physical process. Your favorite childhood memory, what you had for lunch, how you feel about kangaroos, is all embedded in a complex set of physical neural structures in your brain that fire together in a specific pattern. A crude visual is to imagine that each memory is like a tree branch with smaller branches branching off in several directions. Instead of being made of wood, however, they are made of biological cellular material. Your brain is an Amazon forest full of trees and branches, which often fire together to form the complex myriad of thoughts, emotions, memories, and everything else that makes up your mind.

The above concepts and analogies have helped me to reframe my experience with difficult people. After all, when my computer misbehaves or doesn't do what I want it to do, I know that it can only be because of one of two reasons:

1) Bad instructions: I failed to use my computer properly. I didn't give it the right instructions; I didn't click the right buttons in the right order. Theoretically, a solution is always at my fingertips, I am just failing to see it.

2) Impossible instructions: I gave my computer instructions it is not capable of following, either due to hardware, software, or physical limitations. For example, my desktop computer is very smart but it can't bake me a chocolate cake. Unless, of course, I program it to. Even then, it would be a major challenge.

Both points of failure stem from outside of the computer's control. In fact, the computer has no real control over anything. Therefore, when a failure occurs, I do not begrudge or resent my computer. Instead, I examine my interaction with it. Did I click the wrong thing? Did I mistype the URL? Is my computer even capable of doing what I am asking of it?

I apply this same reasoning to my dealings with people. If they don't do what I want them to, I figure it is either because I haven't used the right combination of words, or the person is incapable of doing what I need them to do. Framing the problem in this way has helped me to take ownership and motivate myself in situations that require my attention while, at the same time, to let go of situations that I feel are beyond my influence. It is an emotional hack that speeds up the process of moving forward as opposed to uselessly ruminating on a relationship problem.

## Piecing it Together: Become a Compassionate Monster

My central recommendation in this book is that you should adopt two divergent approaches when dealing with people, depending on their motives and psychologies. The first approach is compassionate. Use this with most people. I have discussed some specific cognitive and behavioral tools that you can adopt to enhance this approach (i.e., meditation, mirroring, non-violent communication, validation, etc.). Most people already know how to be compassionate. After all, most people practice compassion regularly when dealing with their loved ones. The challenge of acting compassionately, therefore, is not borne of a lack of knowledge or experience. Rather, it's a matter of impulse control and concentration. Emotions, circumstances, and poorly systemized incentives can get the better of us. Therefore, few people are able to act compassionately with everyone all the time. Nor is this expected. Instead, the aim ought to be to hone your tools of compassion so that they are more readily available to you than they otherwise would be.

The second approach is competitive and is reserved for use with people that have severe personality disorders (most notably psychopathy) or an innate inability to reciprocate compassion. Most people, especially women, struggle with this approach. This struggle is not due to an inadequacy of some kind. Rather, women on average tend to rate higher on the personality dimension of agreeableness as compared to men. If you're the kind of person that values and practices gentleness, compassion, cooperation, etc., then switching modes into aggression can result in a cognitive dissonance that is jarring and uncomfortable. It's tempting to resolve this dissonance by suppressing and disconnecting from your inner monster. It is an intuitive solution. However, it is also a mistake, as I will explain in the next section.

## Psychopaths Make us Better People

Recall that earlier in this book, I provided two reasons for why it is worthwhile to develop a strategy against psychopaths. The first is that even low probability events are worth mitigating if the potential harm is high and the cost of mitigation is low. The second reason, and the topic of this section, is that this preparation will make you a better person overall.

Learning how to deal with psychopaths provides ancillary benefits worth pursuing. It is analogous to lifting weights in the gym. You don't expect to ever have to squat 135 pounds in your day-to-day life, however, squatting a heavy weight in the gym on a regular basis will help you develop the kind of musculature that will assist you to get out of a chair in your 80s; it will help you burn calories throughout the day; it will help to develop the gray matter in your brain. These are highly worthwhile ancillary benefits. Analogously, learning the skills required to deal with psychopaths will make you a better, more confident person.

Before I proceed on this point, I should clarify what I mean by "aggression". Sometimes people conflate aggression with physical violence. I do not advocate for the use of physical violence. However, I recognize that there are rare circumstances where physical violence is necessary (e.g., self-defense, defense of others, etc.).

Uncontrolled aggression ought to be avoided. Controlled aggression, on the other hand, is a useful tool in limited circumstances. Unprovoked aggression is usually a bad thing. Aggression in response to aggression is sometimes the only available and/or the most optimal path. The human capacity for aggression evolved because it is useful.[11] It is a tool to be used when appropriate. The way to harness this tool is to get to know your dark side.

I subscribe to the view of the likes of the famous psychologist, Carl Jung, who made compelling cases that in order to be an emotionally whole and mature person, we must recognize the parts of our personality that are in shadow (i.e., unconscious). The shadow can hold our traumas, desires, and other repressed and often anti-social tendencies. Ignorance of our shadow is dangerous

---

[11] I am not making the claim that all evolved behaviors are useful. Merely that some are, and that aggression falls into this category.

because it blindsides us when we least expect it. As humans living in a complex social and physical environment, we are constantly challenged by novel situations that could trigger us in a variety of ways. By getting to know our shadow, we can better prepare for the unpredictable situations that lie ahead of us.

So, how do we get to know, harness, and wield the power we hold in our shadow? There are many philosophies on this topic, and I highly recommend reading Jung's work. Different paths and methods will work for different people. Here are three that work for me, and I think will work for many of you:

### 1. Tap Into Your Protective Instincts

Mother bears are interesting. They are well-known for being extremely dangerous and aggressive, especially if you go near their cubs. In some cases, they can even thwart the aggression of a much larger male bear. Yet, mother bears can also be gentle and loving with their cubs. Thus, two disparate and extreme forms of behavior (nurture and aggression) arise out of a single circumstance (caretaking for cubs). Positive emotions and motivations such as love, caring, nurturing, and protectiveness can be harnessed and used in a powerful way.

A case in point is a story that a friend once told me. She said that she used to think of herself as somewhat timid, non-aggressive, fearful of animals, and highly gentle in disposition. Yet, one day when confronted with danger, she discovered a side of herself she didn't even know was there. She recounted to me the story of getting ready to go to her car after a business meeting when, through a window, she saw another woman in the parking lot that was approached by several coyotes. My friend didn't hesitate to act. She went out into the parking lot in an aggressive manner and shouted at the coyotes. The coyotes fled immediately. A potential crisis was averted. The woman thanked her and said that she was surprised to see such a slight woman with a kind face act in such an aggressive manner.[12]

All of us, to one extent or another, have protective instincts. There are people, values, and rules we wish to protect. My suggestion is to tap into your protective instincts when dealing with psychopaths. Think of the other people they might harm. Show them that there is a ferocity in you that you can access to protect yourself and others.

## 2. Invite Physical Suffering Into Your Life

Pain is a great teacher. Those of you that suffer or have suffered from chronic pain likely already know this. This is not to say that pain is always desirable or that your pain is justified because it teaches you things. I acknowledge that there is a fundamental difference between pain that is inflicted on you and that you are powerless to stop versus pain that you can control. Furthermore, I am not going to suggest that you damage your body. Rather, I suggest that you place yourself under safe physical strain and discomfort, on a regular basis. This can be done through exercise, fasting, cold showers, sauna, long-held meditative and/or yoga poses, etc.

Several years ago, I broke one of my molars. The repair required a series of painful procedures, including surgery to adjust the gumline and a root canal. The process took about a year and a half to complete. However, throughout this experience, I was aware that the physical suffering I consistently invited into my life for the past decade before the procedures was immensely important in helping

---

[12] I am not condoning my friend's behavior. And I am not recommending that everyone follow her example. However, whether she made a mistake by shouting at the coyotes is irrelevant to the point I am making, which is that our protective instincts can draw out dormant, and sometimes useful, parts of our personalities.

me get through it, both psychologically and physically. Knowing that I could handle pain made it easier to bear.

Research has shown that pain is highly subjective and varies greatly from person to person and even culture to culture. What might be perceived as a minor nuisance to some could be perceived as very painful to others. The good news is that our capacity to deal with pain and, more importantly, to reframe pain is highly malleable. I learned this early on in my life through my own personal experiences. There have been times, for example, where unbeknownst to me, I had a small adhesive such as tape stuck to my finger and the sensation made me think that I had cut my finger, only to examine it and find that it was not so. The inverse has also happened. That is, I injured parts of my body and did not feel the injuries as pain. Rather, I mistook the sensation for some other thing such as an itch, discomfort, etc. Once I realized I was injured, I began to "feel" the pain.

So, how does embracing pain help you deal with psychopaths? First, willingly enduring physical strain can help us become more psychologically resilient. In turn, psychological resilience can help us cope with psychopaths. Second, by embracing pain, you can remove or largely mitigate your fear of it, simply through the classic technique of habituation. Excessive fear could make us behave in non-rational ways that are counterproductive. When dealing with a psychopath, it is usually best to remain alert and cognitively nimble as opposed to locked-up by fear. Furthermore, if you show fear, you will be targeted and pursued more aggressively. Someone that is not afraid is a more formidable opponent. This having been said, fear can also be useful. That's why it's an evolved response. I discuss this next.

### 3. Use Your Fear, Chihuahua-Style

I love animals and I have learned a lot from them. I particularly love and admire Chihuahuas. I didn't always feel this way. Their small size, buggy eyes, and yappy high-pitch bark doesn't make a good first impression. It took me several years to learn to appreciate this breed.

My relationship with Chihuahuas has taught me some valuable lessons. One of those lessons, which relates to the topic at hand, is that ferocity comes from all shapes and sizes. I have seen Chihuahuas cower large dogs just by advancing forward with confidence. Chihuahuas are good at exuding aggression in, what they perceive to be, a threatening situation. Many people think that Chihuahuas' ferocity is limited to their bark. While this is partly true, their bark is not entirely a bluff.

Chihuahuas are so good at faking aggression that they themselves end up buying into it. The bluff becomes reality. They are like a highly skilled method actor that takes on the personality of her character. And when other dogs back away from their aggression, it only serves to reinforce their distorted reality. In other words, they are lying to themselves, but the lie perpetuates in a cycle of positive feedback until it becomes reality.

What drives their aggression? You guessed it, fear. Fear is a double-edged sword. It can harm you, but it can also help you. I have discussed the detriments of fear throughout this book. Now I would like to acknowledge its benefits. After all, being in a defensive and vulnerable position isn't always a disadvantage. It can elicit strong emotions that manifest into powerful actions.

The problem, however, is that fear is a particularly difficult emotion to wield. If fear becomes overwhelming, it can trigger the well-known fight, flight, or freeze response (three Fs). All three Fs have utility. One F may be more ideal than another depending on the context. Unfortunately, you don't get to choose which response you're going to have because it is not a deliberate cognitive process. Rather, it is an automatic physiological response. However, there are deliberate cognitive processes that you can use to increase the probability that you will use one type of response over another.

One such method is to practice your reaction in the safety of your imagination. You are likely familiar with the concept of visualizing success. Sports psychologists recommend that athletes do this to improve their odds during competition. There are many studies to support this approach. However, it should not be confused with wishful thinking, or the vacuous concept of the Law of Attraction as espoused in books such as The Secret. Simply imagining the result you desire is not sufficient for attaining that result. It's not magic.

Rather, the concept of visualization, when done well, can lead to improvements in the cognitive capacity required to carry out a particular task or a series of sub-tasks. For example, there are studies that have shown that practicing a musical instrument or sport in your mind can lead to similar results as that of physical practice. The reason for this is that our brains are not good at distinguishing real-world events and stimuli from imagined ones and, therefore, it is possible to stimulate neural growth and connections in our brains simply by imagining things. Contrary to what the term implies, muscle memory is in your brain, not your muscles.

This technique of imagining yourself in some predicament and trying to solve it entirely in your imagination is likely something you have already done many times throughout your life with varying degrees of effort and success. It is a cognitive tool that has been useful to humans for as long as we have had imaginations and the ability to anticipate and plan for future events. I think it is partly the reason that people consume stories, particularly in the form of fictional books, shows, and films. All compelling stories contain conflict that is solved or resolved in some way. Just as the stories in our imagination, the stories outside of our minds do not pose a physical risk to us. Thus, the stories we consume serve some of the same functions as our own imaginations but, crucially, without the enormous energy cost. Watching Silence of the Lambs requires less energy than imagining it yourself.

It is no wonder, therefore, that books, shows, and movies about psychopaths are so popular. We are fascinated with them. However, the fascination is not borne of admiration. Most people would state that they are repulsed by psychopaths and the horrific things they do on screen, the page, and in the real world. Yet we like stories about them. Why? Partly because they adequately represent the evil in the world that we wish to prepare for.

In most mainstream stories, the psychopath eventually loses. We like to see that. Not necessarily because we like to watch others fail but rather because we like to see others persevere in the face of hardship. After all, a psychopath's loss is usually the outcome of a protagonist's win. Furthermore, all humans, and some mammals are neurophysiologically wired to derive pleasure from comeuppance.

So, here are some practical suggestions that stem from all this. First, stretch and flex your imagination. I bet it is out of practice. The products and expression of other people's hard work and imagination in the form of media is so ubiquitous and easy to access that it has usurped the role of our own imagination. Although other people's stories are useful, they should not be substituted for our own. In other words, media should be used to augment our imagination, not replace it.

Therefore, my recommendation is to sit in silence, close your eyes, and daydream. Yeah, seriously. If you find this boring, it is all the more reason to do it because, essentially, it means that you are bored with yourself. If you are not engaged and captivated by your own mind, then you have work to do because chances are that your mind bores others too. I think the more you do this, the more interesting you will become, both to yourself and others.

Daydreaming is a skill like any other—practice makes perfect. And although perfection is not a coherent concept in this context, I suggest you practice until you get good at it. You know you have gotten good when you start to look forward to it and when you can generate daydreams that move you emotionally.

Second, once you've sharpened your daydreaming skills, decide on what kind of physiological response (i.e., fight, flight, freeze) you want to have when confronted by a psychopath. In my opinion, the best response to a psychopath is to flee, if possible.[13] If it is not possible, fight. The last thing you want to do is freeze.

Therefore, imagine scenarios where you respond to a psychopath in an optimal manner. Importantly, make it realistic. Do not fantasize about reactions that are well outside your normal behavioral repertoire, such as punching the psychopath across the building like an action hero. Furthermore, what I mean by "fight" does not actually entail any physical fighting (unless you are being physically attacked and there is no escape). In most cases, fight, for me, means assertively standing my ground, speaking directly, being present in my body and exuding a confident physical presence, controlling the tone and vibe of the room, revealing hints of parts of my mind that could be recruited to fight ferociously, if need be, and yet keeping my cool all at the same time.

In a sense, to use fear well against a psychopath, you must hide it and exude confidence.[14] This results in a transformation, from fear to courage. After all, fear and courage are not far apart emotionally (though they often are behaviorally). Rather, they are flip sides of the same coin. Courage always starts out from a place

---

[13] I don't mean bolt out the door like a lunatic when a psychopath enters your office. What I mean is that you should look for ways to minimize or eliminate your interaction with psychopaths.

[14] Showing fear is also useful sometimes, as in when you want to be genuine and vulnerable with someone that cares for you. I'm all for that. Just don't show any vulnerability with a psychopath, even one that claims to love you.

of fear, otherwise, it is not courage—it is stupidity or ignorance. The fine line between stupidity and courage, therefore, is fear.

My sweet loving Chihuahua, aptly named "Tiny" (not by me), practiced her ferocity too, in her sleep. She would dream of her enemies, such as the Pitbull that nearly bit her and the German Shepherd down the road that eyed her nefariously when she passed by. In her sleep, she charges forward and barks. I know this because I hear her muffled bark and I see her little paws moving synchronously as if in mid-run. The movements are subdued, of course, by the glycine-induced paralysis of REM sleep, but they nonetheless reveal her dream to me, or at least some part of it. I gently put my hand on her to wake her and when she opens her eyes, I see a brief flash of her inner power as it transitions from ferocity for her enemies to ferocious love for me. Love too can be ferocious. But that's another topic.

# 5.

# Summary and Final Thoughts

Now that you have familiarized yourself with my way of thinking, some of the research I rely on, and the concepts I have elucidated, I recommend looking back at the table of contents in the beginning of this book. It summarizes my rationale in a hierarchical manner that parallels my thought process fairly well. The meat of this book is contained in sections three and four. These sections describe two fundamentally different ways of dealing with two fundamentally different types of people—regular folks that are in a bad mood and psychopaths.

## "But, Ben, What About Assholes?"

One of the main recurring objections or criticisms I have received about the ideas I have discussed here can be summed up like this: some people's misbehavior cannot be attributed to a bad mood or a personality disorder. Rather, some people are just jerks—perhaps they weren't raised properly, or they live in a tough environment. What do you do with people like this?

My response to this objection is that no one is actually a jerk. If you deal with people compassionately, you will find that **most** people possess a deep capacity for kindness and connection. Some merely have a difficult time accessing that part of themselves. Sometimes this is because they have lived under circumstances that disincentivize kindness and other pro-social expressions.

Furthermore, I acknowledge that different cultures have different norms of behavior, some of which can appear to be aggressive or anti-social to members outside of that culture. However, when it comes to human interaction, I find that there are more similarities than differences between people of different cultures. Or at the very least, there are enough similarities upon which to build common ground and cooperate.

This having been said, note that I emphasized "most". I concede that sometimes people will misbehave in ways that cannot be dealt with. And such people are not necessarily psychopaths. Usually, they are individuals that have been hurt themselves. They were made to feel powerless, and in response to their trauma, they attempt to regain power by overpowering other people, sometimes by any means necessary. Thus, they are engaged in a cycle of suffering. You can attempt to reason with them and use the techniques I discussed in this book but it won't always work.

I have faced individuals like this in my life and failed to reach them. Those types of interactions haunt me more than any other. I find it difficult not to blame myself. After all, I was not able to deescalate the situation. I lacked the skill, depth, and/or knowledge to do so. This is the most comforting way to explain it because the alternative is worse. The alternative is that some people, in some circumstances, at the specific moment in their lives that intersects with mine, cannot be reached no matter my knowledge, skillset, or approach. This is a terrible possibility because it means that it is a problem outside of my influence. Perhaps it cannot be solved through an interpersonal process. It is perhaps a societal problem. And, unfortunately, most societies are not good at dealing with trauma, abuse, bullying, and other forms of cyclical or transferable suffering.

I leave you with this final thought: chances are that you have been a difficult person too at some point in your life. There is no shame in this. On the contrary, it holds the key to growth. Analyze those moments and be mindful of your inner state when this occurs. Let it fuel your own inner wisdom and empathy for others that are occasionally, momentarily, helpless in the grip of an emotion that overrides their better judgement. Practice gentle loving kindness. It really is the ultimate answer.

# About the Author

Ben's first publication, How to Deal With Difficult People, relies on his professional experience and academic background. With nearly 20 years of serial entrepreneurship under his belt, he is involved in multiple business ventures, including his role as founder and CEO at Walk-In Notary. He attained a Psychology degree from the University of Guelph and a law degree from the University of Western Ontario. In addition to his professional and academic interests and achievements, Ben is also a prolific artist, having released many musical, artistic, and other works. He is a deep thinker that seeks to combine seemingly disparate ideas into cohesive frameworks that will help us understand an increasingly complex world. Ben lives in Burlington, Ontario, Canada

Stay in touch at www.projectintrinsic.com

# Thank you

As a thank you for supporting my work, I am pleased to offer you a free audio version of this book. I invite you to share the audiobook with anyone that you think may benefit from it. You can download it from this link: https://subscribepage.io/difficultpeopleaudio or use the QR code below.

Manufactured by Amazon.ca
Bolton, ON

37456964R00037